Leandro Croche

Virtual Reality

Leandro Croche

Virtual Reality

The Feasibility of Total Immersion Today

ScienciaScripts

Imprint

Any brand names and product names mentioned in this book are subject to trademark, brand or patent protection and are trademarks or registered trademarks of their respective holders. The use of brand names, product names, common names, trade names, product descriptions etc. even without a particular marking in this work is in no way to be construed to mean that such names may be regarded as unrestricted in respect of trademark and brand protection legislation and could thus be used by anyone.

Cover image: www.ingimage.com

This book is a translation from the original published under ISBN 978-613-9-62905-3.

Publisher:
Sciencia Scripts
is a trademark of
Dodo Books Indian Ocean Ltd. and OmniScriptum S.R.L publishing group

120 High Road, East Finchley, London, N2 9ED, United Kingdom
Str. Armeneasca 28/1, office 1, Chisinau MD-2012, Republic of Moldova, Europe
Printed at: see last page
ISBN: 978-620-7-75501-1

Summary

Virtual Reality - The Feasibility of Total Immersion Today

Figure 1: Omni, Virtuix immersion accessory

Summary

Virtual reality, once expensive and somewhat inaccessible, is now part of our daily lives. But is total immersion in virtual reality even possible with current technology? The aim of this book, the fruit of research into various sources, is to analyze current Virtual Reality technologies and speculate, based on the information gathered, on the possibility of total immersion in virtual reality. It will also be shown whether such a possibility is being evaluated by development companies. We will do this by first defining what virtual reality is. After this, we will give a brief history of the creation and evolution of virtual reality, showing some milestones in the technology and how these milestones have influenced, through mistakes and successes, the companies currently developing the technology. Based on the studies carried out for this article, we conclude that of the technologies studied, three of them provide the feasibility of total immersion in VR.

Keywords: virtual reality, evolution, technology, total immersion.

1. Introduction - A Brief History

Virtual Reality, also known as immersive multimedia or computer simulated reality, by definition, is a computer technology that replicates an environment, real or imaginary, and simulates the physical presence of a user in a way that allows them to interact with that environment. Virtual reality artificially creates a sensory experience, which can include sight, touch, hearing and smell.

Virtual reality technology, currently seen with hope by major game developers as the one that will bring a great revolution in the player experience, is much older than it seems. In fact, the creation of virtual reality began, as a concept, before the 1950s, in the science fiction work "Pygmalion's Spectacles" by Stanley G. Weinbaum (a short story describing a virtual reality system with a holographic recording of fictional experiences, which included touch and smell) and as a tangible product in 1962, with the manufacture of the Sensorama, built by Morton Heilig.

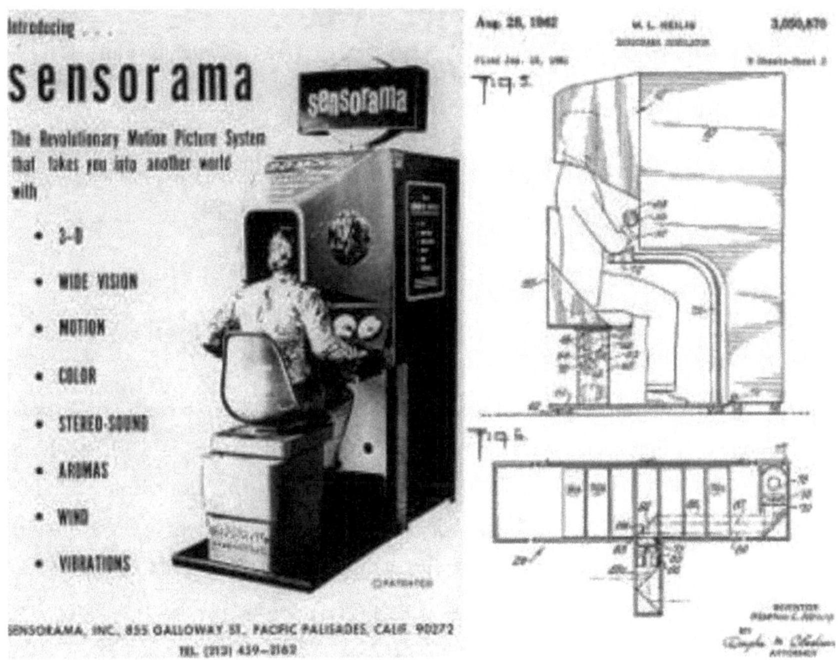

Figure 2: Morton Heilig's sensorama (1962).

The Sensorama was a curious invention for its time. A person would sit in a chair, put their head inside the device (as shown in the picture) and, using glasses built into the device, watch 3D movies, being able to experience stimuli from other senses, such as hearing, touch and smell. The Sensorama can be seen as the first 4D experience in history, and the units that exist today still work.

Jumping forward to 1968, we have what was considered the first virtual reality and augmented reality glasses to be created. The device, called the Sword of Damocles and built by Ivan Sutherland together with his pupil Bob Sproull, was so heavy that it had to be suspended from a cable attached to the ceiling. It was quite primitive in terms of the interface and graphics (which were wire-frame), but it was a big step towards the technology that is used today.

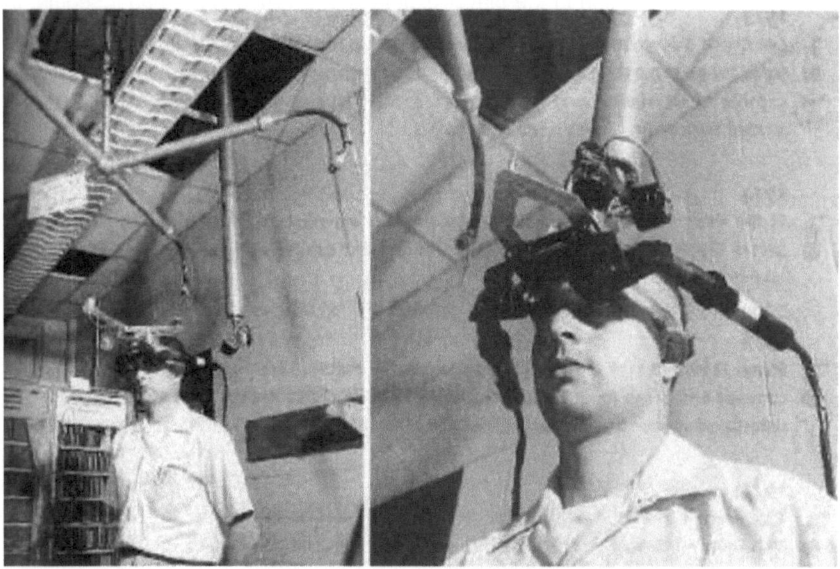

Figure 3 - The Sword of Damocles by Ivan Sutherland and Bob Sproull (1968).

Moving on to 1980, we have the collaboration of Atari, who gave us the arcade Battlezone. Battlezone simulated a first-person tank battle using 3D vector graphics. All you had to do was put your eyes on the screen and control the tank using the levers and buttons available. This is one of the most famous arcade machines ever created by Atari and there are still units in operation today. The Battlezone game will have a reboot for the Sony Playstation 4 and will use the Playstation VR virtual reality glasses. We'll talk about the reboot later.

Figure 4 - Atari's Battlezone arcade (1980).

Figure 5 - The vector graphics of Atari's Battlezone arcade (1980).

Still in the 1980s, with the temporary withdrawal of the American Atari from the video game market, the Japanese developers Nintendo and Sega began a dispute for consumers that is known today as the "Bit Wars" (a pun on Star Wars). The two would also be responsible for manufacturing and distributing VR and virtual immersion technologies for their home consoles in the near future.

Sega would be the first of the two companies to manufacture a virtual reality display. The Sega VR, announced in 1991, made its first appearance in 1993 at the Winter Consumer Electronics Show (Winter CES). Its home version was canceled in 1994, but the Sega VR remained in arcades. The device had LCD screens, stereo headphones and inertial sensors built into its headset, which allowed it to detect the player's movements. Some criticisms related to the fact that prolonged gameplay could cause headaches and dizziness.

Figure 6 - Sega VR by Sega (1993).

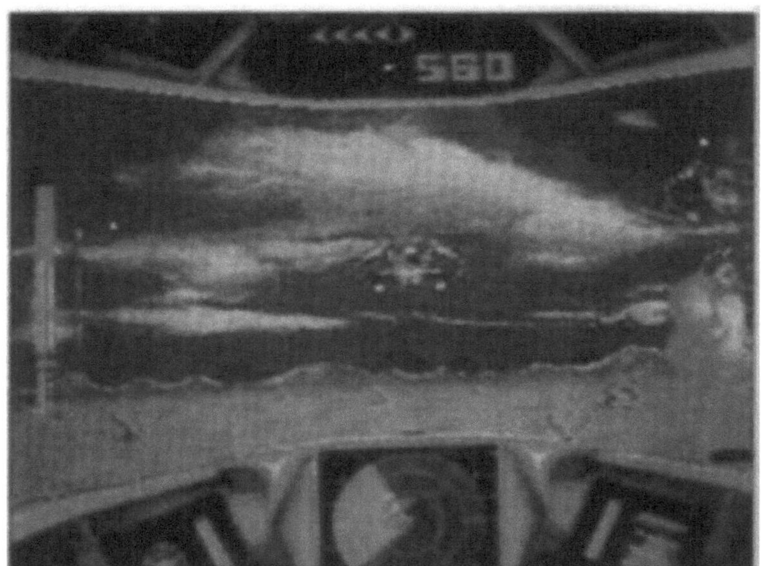

Figure 7 - Nuclear Rush (canceled game) for Sega VR.

Nintendo followed in Sega's footsteps, as you would expect from a competitor, and launched Virtual Boy, its first virtual reality headset, in 1995. Unlike Sega's proposal, Nintendo opted, instead of color graphics on LCD screens, for black and red graphics on LED screens, which were cheaper at the time. The design of the Virtual Boy consisted of a headset on a stand with a controller attached. For all these reasons and a few others, the Virtual Boy was to be a sales and critical failure. The design, which was completely uncomfortable for the player, together with the black and red graphics, which caused headaches and eye pain, were some of the main criticisms of the device. Other complaints were about the price, the variety and quantity of compatible games, since the Virtual Boy was not an accessory like the Sega VR, but a new console, and the lack of immersion in the games (some of them were versions of Super Mario games). Nintendo buried its virtual reality projects after the sales failure and rededicated itself to producing games and new consoles.

Figure 8 - Nintendo's Virtual Boy (1995).

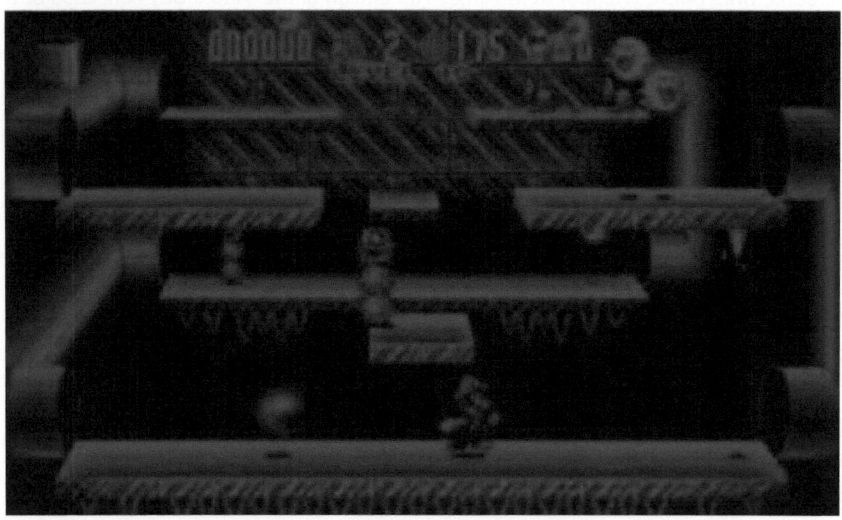

Figure 9 - Mario Clash for Nintendo's Virtual Boy.

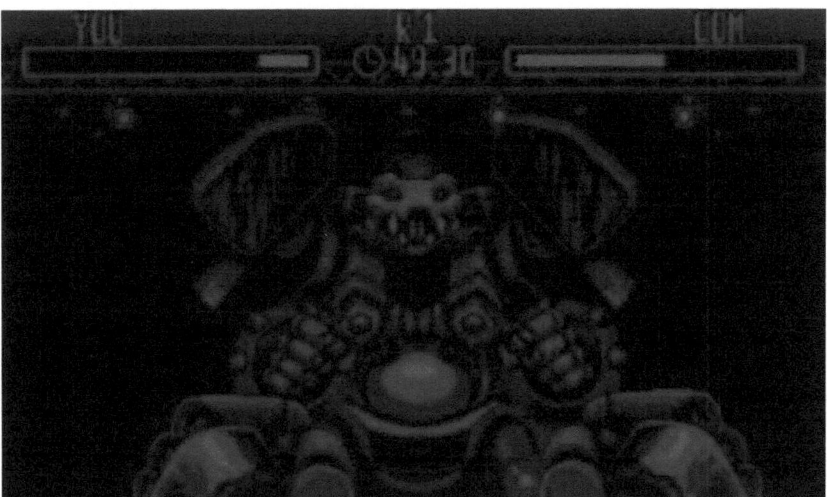

Figure 10 - Teleroboxer for Nintendo's Virtual Boy.

It's worth remembering that the Virtual Boy was mentioned in 2009 on a YouTube channel created by James Rolfe, known on the Internet as AVGN, or Angry Video Game Nerd. He did a full review of the device, highlighting its weaknesses in an amusing way and showing the reasons why the Virtual Boy became a failure at the time of its launch.

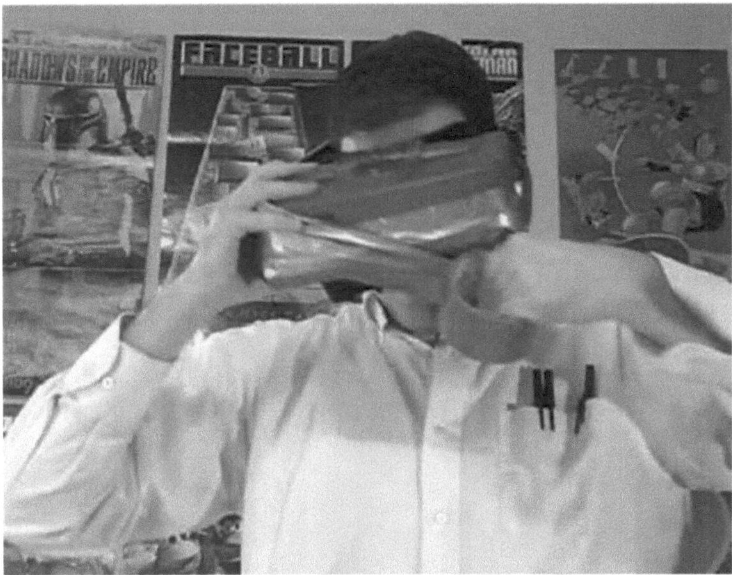

Figure 11 - James Rolfe (or AVGN), in his review of Nintendo's Virtual Boy (2009).

The development of virtual reality technology and immersion in a virtual environment for home consoles was put on the back burner for a while because it was expensive and not very accessible. It remained in arcades and was used in flight and war simulators.

Figure 12: Cockpit of Simcom's Eclipe-500-Simulator, inside view.

Figure 13: Cockpit of Simcom's Eclipe-500-Simulator, external view.

Figure 14: Virtual Reality used in a parachute jump simulation.

However, with the arrival in 2013 of the eighth generation of home consoles and the natural evolution of personal computer hardware and software, virtual reality and immersion technology would once again become relevant. Before we talk about the latest VR technologies, let's talk about virtual immersion.

2. Virtual Reality Immersion

Immersion in virtual reality, by definition, is the perception of being physically present in a non-physical world. This perception is created by surrounding the VR user with images, sounds and other stimuli that provide the sensation of being in a total environment.

Complete immersion in VR is directly related to increased suspension of disbelief. Suspension of disbelief is achieved through stimulation of the five senses - sight, hearing, touch, smell and taste. The more realistic the stimuli in the five senses, the greater the suspension of disbelief and the greater the immersion in VR.

Immersion in VR, therefore, cannot be achieved entirely with headsets containing images and sound, combined with controls with levers and buttons, in an environment in which the player is seated. The whole body must be stimulated for immersion to be achieved. Special accessories, then, combined with motion detection systems, must be added to the experience to achieve a greater level of immersion.

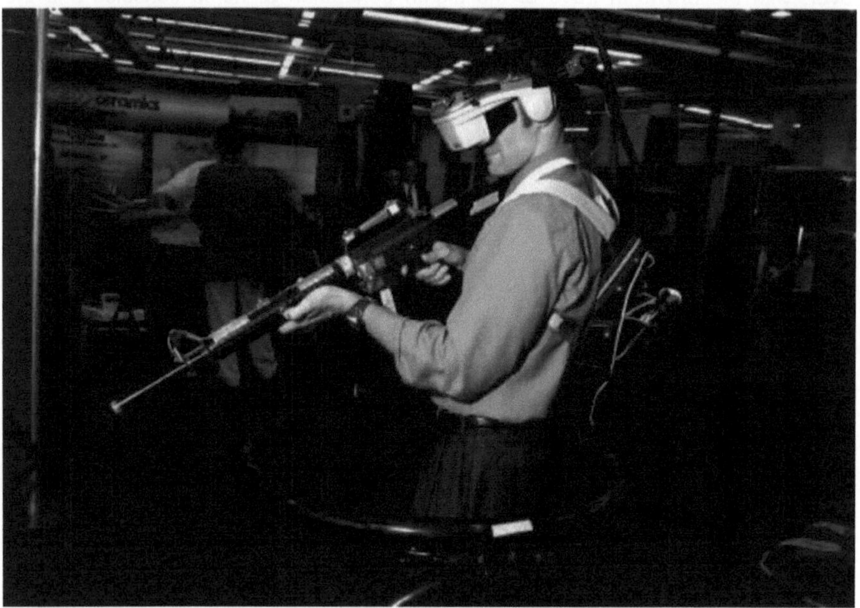

Figure 15: Immersive virtual reality technology.

Considering the history of home consoles and arcades, we have several examples of accessories that provide an immersive experience on one level or another. We'll mention some of the most important and famous.

The Light Guns, which appeared in the 1980s, are a classic and primitive example of immersion. With the Light Gun, you could shoot at your TV screen and hit specific targets. On the Master System, you could add 3D glasses to the experience, which increased the immersion a little more. Practically all consoles up to the 128-bit generation (Playstation 2 and Dreamcast, for example) have a Light Gun and compatible games.

Figure 16: Phaser Gun and 3D Glasses from Sega's Master System (1987/ 1989).

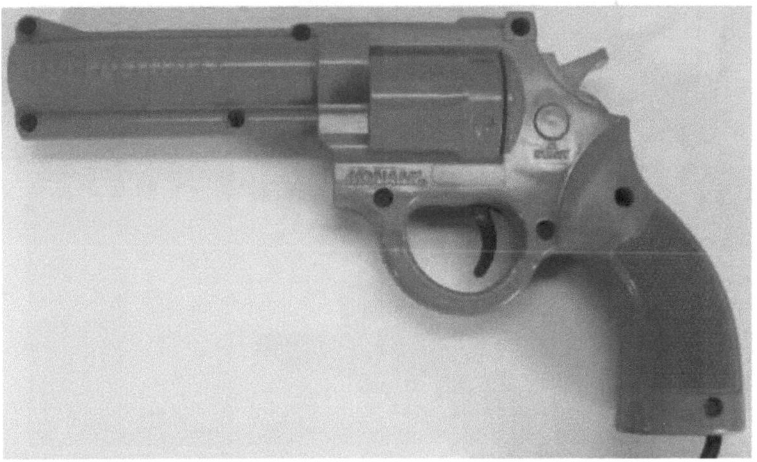

Figure 17: Konami's Justifier, for use on Sega's Mega Drive.

Nintendo's Power Glove, launched in 1989 for use on the Nintendo Entertainment System (or NES), is another famous and primitive immersion accessory. Seen more as an experiment than an accessory in itself, it had few games made specifically for it (a total of four) and was inaccurate in most of the games for which it was compatible. It worked in conjunction with motion sensors that had to be attached around the TV. It appeared in the 1989 film The Wizard (O Gènio do Video Game).

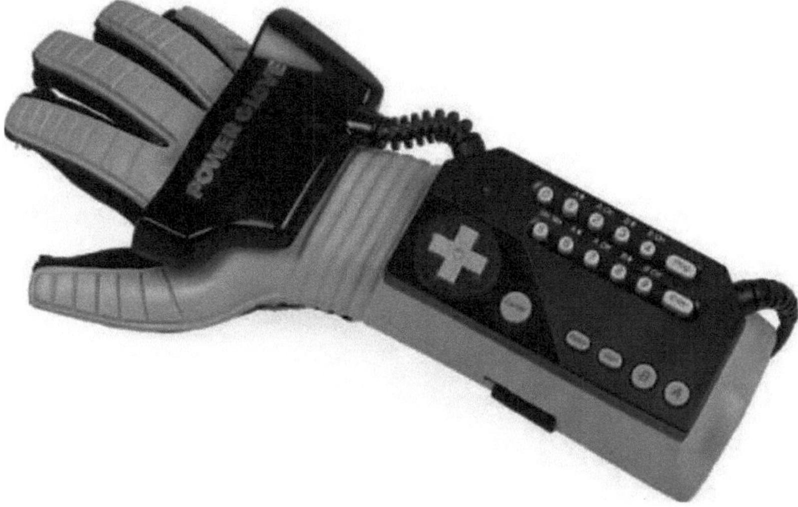

Figure 18: Nintendo Power Glove (1989).

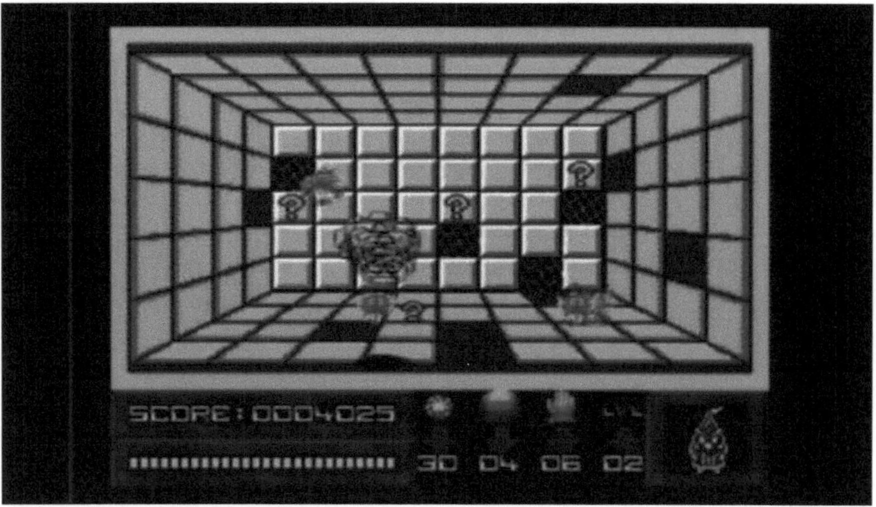

Figure 19: Super Glove Ball for Nintendo's NES, a game specifically for the Power Glove accessory.

Going a little further back in time, we have a less famous but very interesting example. The game Steel Battalion, for Microsoft's Xbox, released in 2002, came with a specific controller that replicated and expanded the mech simulation experience. The controller has several buttons and two levers and pedals and is so large that it has to be rested on a table to make the experience more enjoyable. As an immersive accessory, it was very well received by the media, despite its complexity, number of buttons to perform actions in the game and price.

Figure 20: Steel Battalion for Microsoft Xbox and its specific controller (2002).

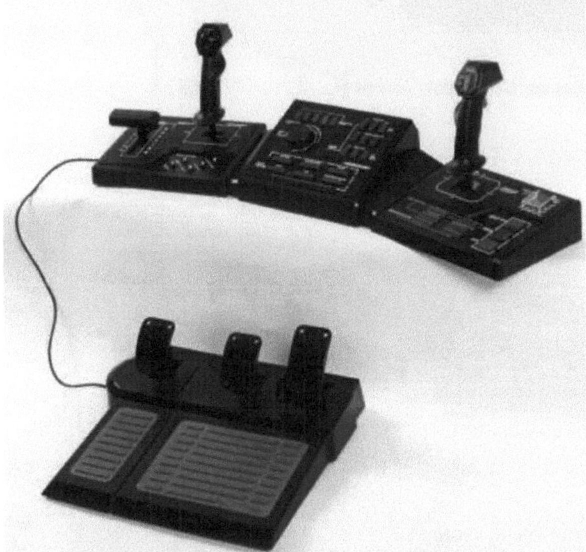

Figure 21 : The specific controller for Steel Battalion, from Microsoft's Xbox (2002).

Two more examples are worth mentioning and will be placed together because of their similarity. The Wii-Mote for Wii (2006) and the Playstation Move (2010) for Playstation 3 and Playstation 4 are accessories that work together with motion sensors to detect players' actions in the real world and transfer them to the game. Playstation Move was launched as an alternative to compete with Xbox 360's Kinect, which uses a camera to detect the player's movements and doesn't need any other accessories. Playstation Move can be used on Playstation 4 to expand the VR experience, combined with Playstation VR.

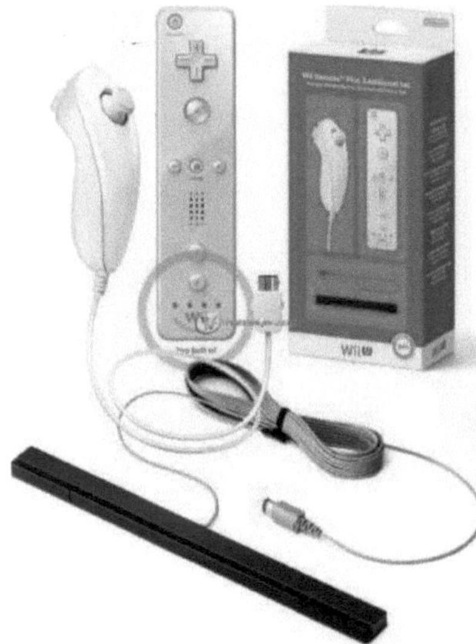

Figure 22: Nintendo's Wii Mote and Sensor Bar (2006).

Figure 23: Sony's Playstation Move and Eyetoy (2010).

All the accessories presented provide immersive experiences on various levels, although they don't work in conjunction with VR (except for Playstation Move). Next, we'll talk about current VR technologies and the immersive accessories that can be used with them, and we'll address the issue of total immersion and the future of virtual reality in the games industry.

3.   Virtual Reality today

With the development of technology and the arrival of the eighth generation of home consoles, virtual reality has become viable again and is now seen as the great hope for game developers. After so many sequels, games with similar and repetitive gameplay, the inclusion of VR comes as a breath of fresh air in the player experience.

There are basically three lines of devices and accessories for use in VR: the proprietary ones (Sony and Microsoft), the multi-platform ones (from Oculus and others for PCs, etc.) and those for smartphones (Samsung, Google, among others). We'll evaluate each of them below.

4. 4. Sony Playstation VR

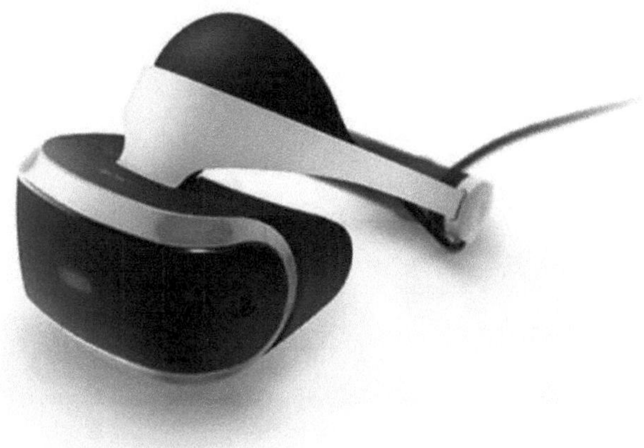

Figure 24: Sony's Playstation VR (2016).

Type: Proprietary (Sony manufacturer; for PS4).

Release date: October 2016.

Expected price: US$ 400.00 (USA).

Specifications:

5.7-inch screen;

1920XRGBx1090 resolution;

120Hz refresh rate;

Field of vision of approximately 100°; Accelerometer, gyroscope, positioning system with nine LEDs, 3D audio, HDMI and USB inputs.

The Playstation VR has VR functionalities, has specific games in production (they will be presented below), works in conjunction with the PS4's Eyetoy and its games can be played with the system's controller or with Playstation Move, to add to the immersive experience.

However, the accessory has some cons. The headset is not built-in like the Oculus Rift and must be purchased separately. Sony recommends using its Pulse 7.1 headset for a more immersive experience. This headset costs around R$ 650.00 in Brazil.

The main games to be produced for the accessory are:

Star Wars Battlefront

Figure 25: Star Wars Battlefront for Sony PS4.

Star Wars Battlefront is a first-person shooter that is an obvious choice for the Playstation VR accessory. There are no further details on how the gameplay will work and which immersive accessories will be compatible.

Rigs Mechanized Combat League

Figure 26: Rigs Mechanize Combat League for Sony PS4.

Rigs is an online multiplayer first-person shooter in which the objective is to join a team of robot pilots in an arena and battle other teams in the quest for victory. It can be played with the Playstation VR goggles and has support for the system controller. It cannot be used with other accessories, such as Move.

EVE Valkyrie

Figure 27: EVE Valyrie for Sony Playstation 4.

Eve Valkyrie is a space combat simulator where you control a ship on a large battlefield in space. With the Playstation VR, you can look around and lock your sights to fire projectiles at your enemies. System control is supported. EVE Valkyrie will also be available for PC, with support for the Oculus Rift.

London Heist

Figure 28: London Heist for Sony Playstation 4.

London Heist is a first-person shooter game that supports Playstation Move and, for this very reason, offers the most immersive and realistic experience. With Playstation Move, you can aim your weapon, shoot and simulate the reloading movement of an automatic pistol. You can also interact with the environment and pick up or move various objects. While shooting, you can also duck and hide, using balconies and other areas as cover. Of all the games shown by Sony, this is one that provides the most immersive and tense experience.

The Deep

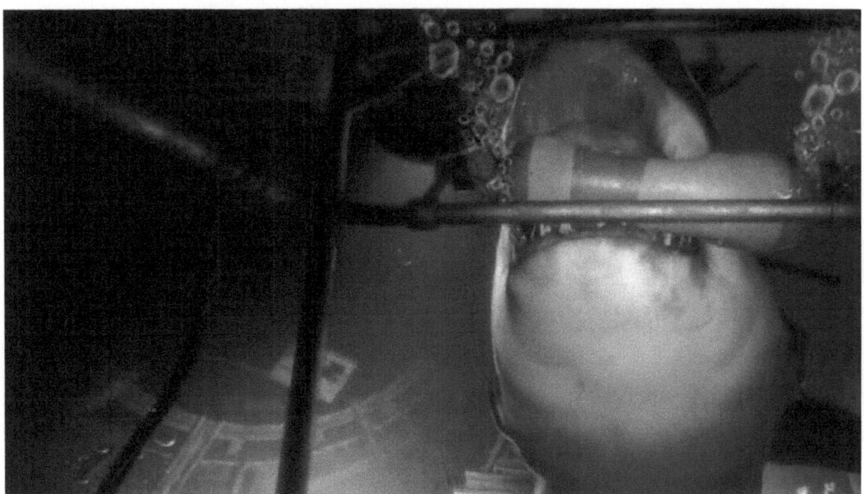

Figure 29: The Deep for Sony's Playstation 4.

The Deep is a very interesting immersive experience. You take on the role of a diver in a cage that is descending towards the bottom of the sea. Using Playstation Move, you can interact with underwater life and one scene is particularly striking: a shark, which is constantly circling the cage, starts attacking it and biting the oxygen tubes attached to it. Like London Heist, it is one of the most intense immersive experiences to be shown by Sony.

Battlezone

Figure 30: Battlezone for Sony's Playstation 4.

Remember Atari's Battlezone arcade, mentioned a few pages above? This is the reboot of the arcade classic, and offers a similar experience, but superior in many ways. Battlezone is a tank war simulator. In the game, you can use Playstation VR to look around and get a more comprehensive idea of the environment. The game supports system control.

Conclusion

In terms of immersion, Playstation VR does a satisfactory but incomplete job. The Playstation VR + Playstation Move combination manages to encompass the senses of sight, hearing and touch, the latter of which is incompletely stimulated. Games such as London Heist have to be played standing up and the Playstation 4's Eyetoy is able to detect movements such as bending down and standing up. However, it is not possible to move forwards, backwards or sideways. The experience is immersive, but still incomplete.

In games that use the system's standard control, you can move in any direction with the directional levers, but you can play sitting down and, in this sense, immersion is partially impaired.

So far, Sony has no plans to launch other accessories to enhance the VR immersion experience. But it is believed that the company will invest in this, provided that Playstaton VR delivers the expected return.

5. Oculus Rift

Figure 31: Oculus Rift.

Type: Multiplatform (Manufacturer Oculus; for PCs and XboxOne)

Release date: March 28, 2016 (already available).

Price: US$ 599.00 (USA)/ R$ 2,400.00 (Brazil).

Specifications:

5.6-inch OLED screen;

Combined resolution of 2160 x 1200 pixels, viewed through dual lenses;

90Hz refresh rate;

Field of vision of 90 degrees horizontal and 110 diagonal;

Built-in 3D audio headphones.

Weight: 470g.

The Oculus Rift is a versatile and comfortable accessory manufactured by Oculus, with a satisfactory resolution that can be used on PCs and is also compatible with the Xbox One. It has a built-in 3D audio headset, which is an advantage over the Playstation VR, for which the headset must be purchased separately.

The most interesting aspect of the Oculus Rift is its compatibility with controllers and many other immersive accessories (such as Virtuix's Omni, which will be presented later), which improves the experience for the player.

The Oculus Rift is not only compatible with games. There is a wide range of media that can be used with the headset, which expands the usefulness of the accessory.

Of all the headsets, the Oculus Rift seems to be the one with the most advantages and the greatest compatibility with different systems.

One point that can be highlighted as a drawback is that it doesn't have the Augmented Reality experience. If you want AR on the Oculus Rift, you'll need front-facing cameras on the headset.

Here are some games made for the Oculus Rift.

Adrift (Adr1ft)

Figure 32: Adr1ft for PC from 505 Games.

Adrift is a first-person exploration game in which the player takes on the role of an astronaut trapped in a destroyed space station. The aim is to create an immersive and suffocating experience, along the lines of the movie Gravity. It is a multiplatform game and has support for each console controller.

Chronos

Figure 33: Chronos for PC by Gunfire Games.

Chronos is a third-person action game that replicates the patient and precise combat experience of From Software's Souls series. As an immersive experience, it doesn't offer anything new, but it is one of the games compatible with the Oculus Rift. For the game, it is recommended that you use the traditional PC controls.

Radial G - Racing Revolved

Figure 34: Radial G Racing Revolved for PC from Team Bio.

Radial G Racing Revolved is a futuristic racing game in which your vehicle is stuck on a cylindrical track. The vehicle can move around the entire length of the track and pick up power-ups that increase its speed. As an immersive experience, it's quite interesting, and gives a distinct feeling of speed. Standard PC controls are supported.

As previously mentioned, the Oculus Rift is compatible with various immersive accessories. We'll mention three of the most important below.

Oculus Touch

Figure 35: Oculus Touch.

The Oculus Touch, an accessory also manufactured by Oculus, is basically a controller, divided so that each hand can use it independently, with built-in motion sensors, which allow the hands to be detected and interact with the VR independently, making the experience more immersive. It should be used in conjunction with two motion detectors, which work in conjunction with the Oculus Touch's built-in sensors.

Peregrine Wearable Interface

Figure 36: The Peregrine Wearable Interface glove.

Gloves for virtual reality interaction are a very common and effective accessory. They can be purchased on Amazon for around US$150.00.

Omni by Virtuix

Figure 37: Omni from Virtuix.

This, of all the immersive accessories, is one of the most interesting. The Omni, combined with other accessories such as the Trinity VR Magnum, a pistol for first-person shooter games and the Oculus Rift, is capable of generating the ultimate immersive experience. The price is US$ 699.00, but other items must be purchased, such as the shoes used to step on the base of the device. All the other items together cost around US$ 380.00.

Conclusion

As we can see, the Oculus Rift and all the accessories that are compatible with it are capable of generating a more immersive virtual reality experience than the Playstation VR, for example. The three most important senses - sight, hearing and touch - are stimulated to the full, provided you have the right accessories. Many more accessories will be available in the future, giving gamers more options and probably putting the Oculus Rift at the top of the list of virtual reality devices.

6. HTC Vive

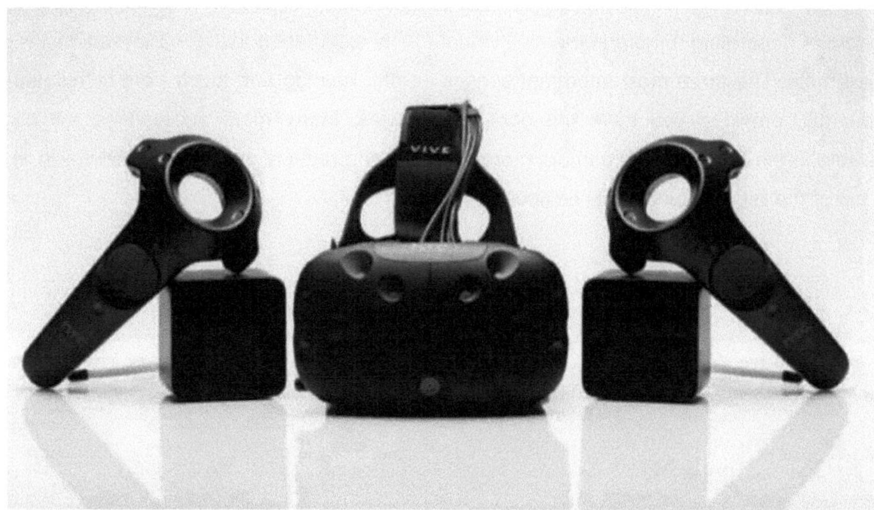

Figure 38: HTC's HTC Vive.

Type: Multiplatform (Manufacturer HTC/Valve; for PCs)

Release date: April 5, 2016 (already available).

Price: US$ 799.00 (USA).

Specifications:

5.6-inch OLED screen;

1920 x 1080 pixel resolution for each lens;

90Hz refresh rate;

110° field of vision;

Weight: 555g.

HTC Vive, the virtual reality and augmented reality headset resulting from the joint work between HTC and Valve, is considered by many to be the device that brings the most accurate VR experience. The controls with built-in sensors that come with the device, and which work in conjunction with the detectors, give the user an experience that is both immersive and precise. It also has a system that scales the environment and uses it in the VR experience. This works via the sensors built into the headset, in conjunction with the detectors that come with the device.

The three negative points of the HTC Vive, justified by those who have tried the device, are: it needs a large room to install its detection systems and for the user to move around; it has a long wire, which can get in the way of the experience, since it can get in the way when the user is moving around, causing them to trip and the device does not have built-in headphones, requiring the consumer to purchase them separately.

Figure 39: User using HTC Vive.

Below are some games presented for the HTC Vive, which use its sensor detection and control systems.

The Gallery: Call of the Starseed

Figure 40: The Gallery: Call of the Starseed by Cloudhead Games.

The Gallery is an episodic first-person exploration game in which you have to enter a fantasy world in search of your lost sister. According to its developers, it makes full use of the environment's scaling system to provide a more immersive experience.

Elite: Dangerous

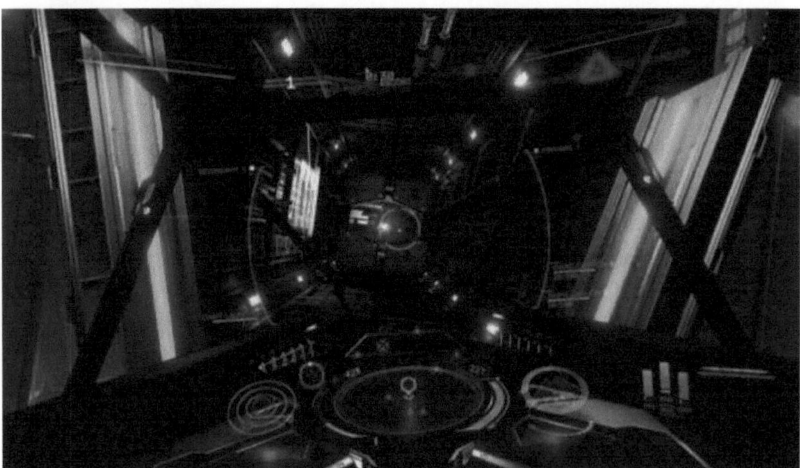

Figure 41: Elite: Dangerous by Frontier.

Elite: Dangerous is a multiplayer space combat simulation game, previously released for the Oculus Rift, now prioritized for the Vive. Strangely enough, it's a traditional game in which the player must remain seated to enjoy the experience.

Vanishing Realms

Figure 42: Vanishing Realms by Indimo Labs.

Vanishing Realms is a first-person exploration and melee combat game in which you have to explore a fantastic environment and fight enemies using swords and shields. It uses the Vive's sensor controls to create a precise and immersive combat experience.

Space Pirate Trainer VR

Figure 43: Space Pirate Trainer VR by I-Illusions.

Space Pirate Trainer VR is a first-person shooter in which the aim is to shoot at targets, which appear from all sides, and get the most points. According to those who have tested it, it's fun and addictive and the Vive's controls provide precision and immersion in the experience.

Hover Junkers

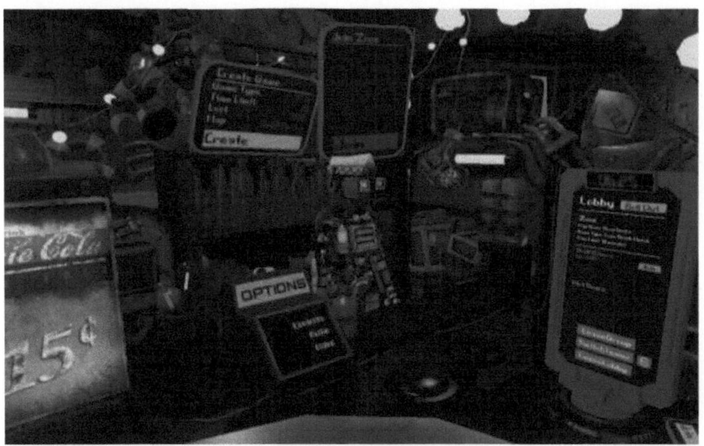

Figure 44: Hover Junkers from Stress Level Zero.

Hover Junkers is a first-person multiplayer combat game in which the Vive's scanning and scaling system uses the environment you're in to create the game's atmosphere and you can fight other players by shooting with the controls and hiding behind walls created by the scanning system.

Conclusion

The HTC Vive is a very interesting VR immersion device and offers an immersive experience without the need for other accessories that have to be purchased separately. Several games have been released and are available on Steam and others are on the way.

7. Hololens

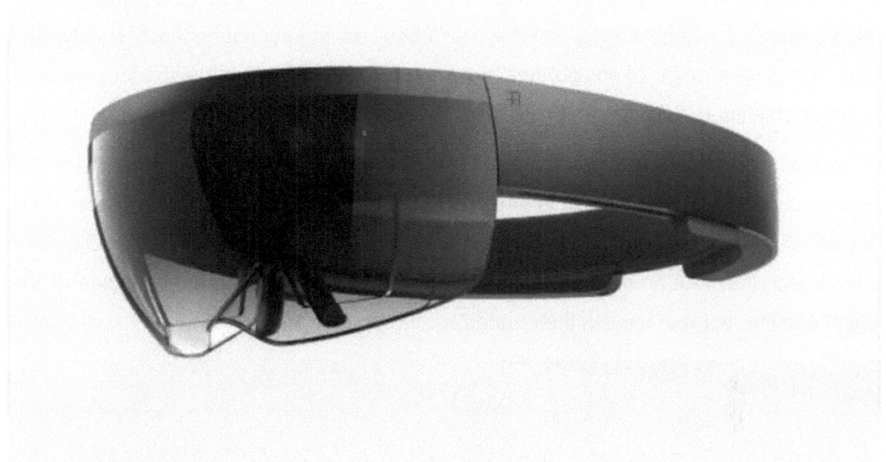

Figure 45: Microsoft Hololens.

Type: Multiplatform (Manufacturer Microsoft; for PCs and systems using Android, IOS and OSX)

Release Date: Developer version already available. Consumer version to be announced.

Price: US$ 3,000.00 (USA).

Specifications:

32-bit Intel processor;

Holographic processor (HPU) customized by Microsoft itself;

2GB RAM, 64GB internal memory;

Wi-Fi, Bluetooth, Micro-USB input;

4 external cameras for the device to capture the entire environment, 1 2MP camera capable of recording HD videos and capturing photos, 4 microphones to capture the user's voice and commands;

Several sensors, including a proximity sensor (which is combined with a camera) and another capable of measuring inertia;

Weight: 579g.

Microsoft's Hololens is a little different from its competitors. Microsoft's Hololens is not a virtual reality immersion accessory, but an augmented reality accessory, using the environment as a backdrop, adding objects and information to interact with and displaying them on the device's holographic display. And the most interesting thing is that it doesn't use other immersion accessories, just the user's body as an information input. This type of feature opens up a range of possibilities, covering not only games, but also other types of experience relating to teaching and medicine, for example.

Two presentations made with the Hololens deserve a mention, as they demonstrate the headset's capabilities. The first Hololens presentation to be mentioned took place at E3 2015, with the game Minecraft. The Hololens user can visualize the entire construction of a city in Minecraft in real time, anywhere they want, through the holographic lenses of the headset and interact with it using their hands.

Figure 46: Hololens and Minecraft - Presentation at E3 2015.

The other Hololens presentation was of a game called Project X-Ray. The user of the headset uses the room he is in as a backdrop and enemies appear from all directions. The user uses an immersion accessory to shoot at the enemies and interact with them in different ways.

Figure 47: User using Microsoft's Hololens in the Project X-Ray presentation.

Currently, only the developer version of Hololens is available. The release date for the consumer version has yet to be announced, but it's a promising device and promises to revolutionize the augmented reality experience.

8. Samsung Gear VR

Figure 48: Samsung Gear VR.

Type: Smartphone accessory (Manufacturer Samsung/Oculus; for Samsung Galaxy Note 5, S6 and S7 smartphones).

Release Date: November 27, 2015 (Already available).

Price: R$ 799.00.

Specifications:

96°w field of vision;

Accelerometer, Gyroscope, Magnetic, Proximity;

Photon movement latency: < 20 ms;

Interpupillary distance coverage: 55 ~ 71 mm;

Touch pad, back button, volume key;

Dimensions: 198 (W) x 116 (L) x 90 (H) mm;

MicroSD card (16 GB);

5.7-inch Quad HD Super AMOLED (143.9 mm) 2560 x 1440 resolution;

High frame rate preview (60 fps);

Spatial Sound 3D in Samsung VR Player for VR Gallery content;

Weight: 318g.

The Samsung Gear VR is a comfortable and lightweight accessory that allows you to attach your Samsung smartphone to get a virtual reality experience, which applies to both games and other media, such as movies. At the same time as it is seen as a quality product by many users, with games that surprise with their graphics, sound and gameplay quality, considering that they work on a smartphone, there is no shortage of criticism, some of which is directed at the high price of the accessory, bearing in mind that it does not itself provide any VR experience and depends on a smartphone to do so. Other complaints concern the fact that the Samsung Gear is not compatible with other smartphone brands and there are also consumers who claim that the VR experience is not very different from holding the smartphone close to your face.

The Samsung Gear VR must be used in conjunction with a Bluetooth controller. Samsung recommends using its proprietary controller, but other brands are also compatible.

Figure 49: Samsung Controller.

Figure 50: Stratus XL from Steelseries.

The accessory does not have headphones attached, which must be purchased separately by the user; it has focus adjustment and volume adjustment on the top and side respectively; it draws power directly from the smartphone for its own operation. It has no other immersion accessories apart from the bluetooth controls.

Samsung has its own store for purchasing titles for use with the Samsung Gear VR, called VR Oculus. Here are some games compatible with the Samsung Gear VR.

EVE Gunjack

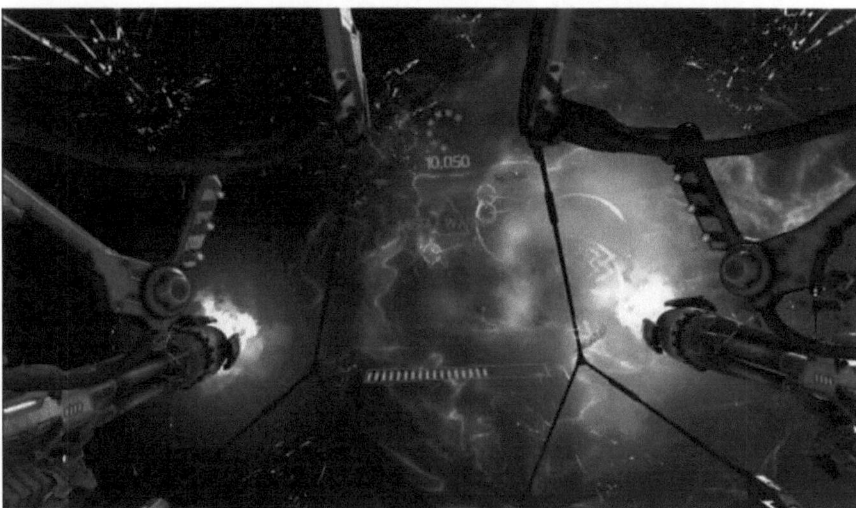

Figure 51: EVE Gunjack by CCP Games.

From the same producer as EVE Valkyrie and EVE Online, EVE Gunjack is a first-person space combat simulation game that uses the Samsung Gear VR for a more immersive experience and must be played with bluetooth controls. It has a more arcade gameplay focus and surprises with its graphic quality. It is also available for use with HTC Vive and Oculus Rift.

Land's End

Figure 52: Land's End by Ustwo.

Land's End is a first-person exploration and puzzle-solving game. It's very relaxing, immersive and minimalist in its visuals.

Dreadhalls

Figure 53: Dreadhalls from White Door Games.

Dreadhalls is a first-person horror and exploration game that makes good use of the

Samsung Gear VR and its controls. It's easy to get tense with the atmosphere the game provides. Also available for the Oculus Rift.

Conclusion

The Samsung Gear VR provides a VR immersion option for owners of a Samsung smartphone, but that's about it. The immersion is reasonably satisfactory, but incomplete, and depends a lot on the smartphone you have. It may disappoint the most demanding, who expect a differentiated and immersive experience, but it surprises those who just want one more option to have fun using their Samsung smartphone.

9. Google Cardboard VR

Figure 54: Google Cardboard.

There's not much to say about Google Cardboard other than that it's priced at US$15.00 on Google's official website and that it's a smartphone adapter for providing the virtual reality experience. It can be used with any type of smartphone and is a cheap option compared to its competitors.

It's worth mentioning for having sold millions of copies worldwide and for drawing Google's attention to the reality market. They are thinking of opening a virtual reality division and manufacturing plastic versions of the adapter.

10. Case Study

	Oculus Rift	HTC Vive	Playstation VR	Hololens	Samsung Gear VR	Google Cardboard VR
Name Manufacturer	Oculus VR	HTC, Valve	Sony	Microsoft	Samsung	Google
Screen	2x OLED	2x OLED	OLED	Holographic lens	Amoled	Depends on the smartphone
Resolution	2160x1200px (combined lenses)	2160x1200px (combined lenses)	1920x1080px (combined lenses)	1268x720px (each lens)	2560x1440px (combined lenses)	Depends on the smartphone
Frame Rate	90fps	90fps	120fps	30fps	60fps	Depends on the smartphone
Field of vision	>110°	>110°	100°	90°	96°	90°
Control	Xbox One controller	Two SteamVR controllers, one for each hand	DualShock 4	No need	Samsung Controller	Various controls
Weight	470g	555g	610g	579g	318g	40g
Audio	Built-in, but can be removed and replaced	External	External	Built-in	External	External
Requirements	High-performance computer	High-performance computer	PlayStation 4	No need for another device (built-in processor)	Samsung Galaxy Note 5, S6, S7	A smartphone
Release Date	March 28, 2016	April 05, 2016	October/2016	Developer version already available / Consumer version to be announced	November 27th 2015	June 24, 2014
Price	US$ 599,00 (USA) /R$ 2.400,00 (BRA)	US$ 799,00 (USA)	US$ 400,00 (USA)	US$ 3.000,00 (USA) - developer version	R$ 799,00	US$ 15,00
Compatibility with Immersion Accessories	Compatible with multiple immersion accessories (examples: Oculus Touch, Peregrine Weareble Interface, Omni by Virtuix etc.)	Only compatible with native accessories	PlayStation Move	Uses the user's body as a control and has accessories to be announced	No	No
Is total immersion feasible?	Yes	Yes	No	Yes, but it's a different kind of immersion (Augmented Reality)	No	No

11. Qualitative Analysis of Virtual Reality Headsets - Technical Characteristics and Feasibility of Total Immersion

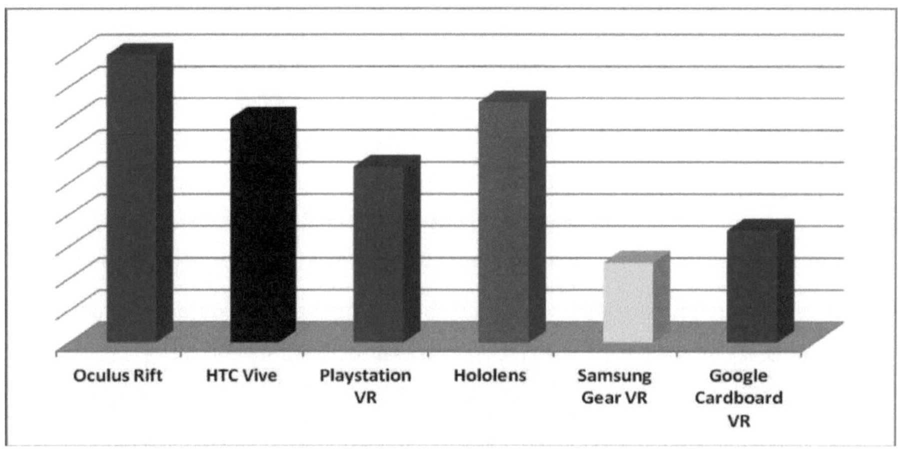

The analysis above considers and weighs up the items in the headsets table. The Oculus Rift is the big winner, as it manages to beat its competitors in the combination of categories compatibility with accessories, resolution, versatility, price and total immersion feasibility. The Hololens comes in second place and beats its competitors in the categories of built-in audio, total immersion feasibility and processing hardware built into the headset, but loses out in terms of resolution. The HTC Vive comes third, losing out to the Hololens only in the areas of minimum hardware for the headset to work (which, in the case of the Vive, is external to the headset) and interaction with virtual reality (which, in the case of the Hololens, doesn't require accessories and, in the case of the Vive, requires two controls, one in each hand).

The Playstation VR loses out in the categories of total immersion in VR, resolution, weight and accessory compatibility (it only allows the use of the Playstation VR). Samsung VR and Google Cardboard VR don't stand a chance against their competitors, as they are just accessories that need a smartphone (which is much more expensive and adds to the price of the accessories) to work. Google Cardboard VR beats Samsung Gear VR because it's cheaper and lighter.

12. Final considerations

In conclusion, total immersion in VR is currently feasible, but expensive, as long as you buy all the accessories for it.

Of all the headsets analyzed (see comparative table and graph attached above), the only ones that manage to replicate a completely immersive VR experience are the Oculus Rift, the Hololens and the HTC Vive. The Oculus Rift has the advantage of being more versatile and having more accessories available, the Hololens is very promising, doesn't need immersive accessories and also has a lot to offer compared to its competitors and the Vive has more advanced technology and has more functions that can be explored in the future.

The future holds great surprises when it comes to virtual reality and augmented reality technology, given what the market and developers currently have to offer.

13. Bibliography

WIKIPEDIA, Virtual Reality at: <https://en.wikipedia.org/wiki/Virtual_reality>, accessed April 30, 2016.

WIKIPEDIA, Immersion (Virtual Reality) in:

<https://en.wikipedia.org/wiki/Immersion_(virtual_reality)>, accessed April 30, 2016.

WIKIPEDIA, Immersive Technology in:

<https://en.wikipedia.org/wiki/Immersive_technology>, accessed on April 30, 2016.

WIKIPEDIA, Playstation VR at: <https://en.wikipedia.org/wiki/PlayStation_VR>, accessed April 30, 2016.

WIKIPEDIA, Oculus Rift at: <https://en.wikipedia.org/wiki/Oculus_Rift>, accessed April 30, 2016.

WIKIPEDIA, HTC Vive at: <https://en.wikipedia.org/wiki/HTC_Vive>, accessed April 30, 2016.

WIKIPEDIA, Microsoft HoloLens in:

<https://en.wikipedia.org/wiki/Microsoft_HoloLens>, accessed on April 30, 2016.

WIKIPEDIA, Samsung Gear VR in:

<https://en.wikipedia.org/wiki/Samsung_Gear_VR>, accessed on April 30, 2016.

WIKIPEDIA, Google Cardboard at: <https://en.wikipedia.org/wiki/Google_Cardboard>, accessed April 30, 2016.

ROLFE, JAMES, Virtual Boy - Angry Video Game Nerd - Episode 42, at: <https://www.youtube.com/watch?v=OyVAp0tOk5A>, accessed April 30, 2016.

VIRTUIX, OMNI - at: <http://www.virtuix.com/products/>, accessed April 30, 2016.

PRASUETHSUT, LILY - The best HTC Vive games you need to play - in: <http://www.wareable.com/vr/best-steam-vr-games>, accessed April 30, 2016.

CHARARA, SOPHIE - Best Samsung Gear VR apps: The games, videos and experiences to download first - <http://www.wareable.com/vr/best-samsung-gear-vr- apps-the-games-demos-and-experiences-to-download-first-816>, accessed April 30, 2016.

STATT, NICK - Microsoft's HoloLens explained: How it works and why it's different - <http://www.cnet.com/news/microsoft-hololens-explained-how-it-works-and-why-its-

different/>, accessed April 30, 2016.

PINO, NICK - HTC Vive Review - <http://www.techradar.com/reviews/wearables/htc- vive-1286775/review>, accessed April 30, 2016.

RUBIN, PETER - Review: Oculus Rift - <http://www.wired.com/2016/03/oculus-rift- review-virtual-reality/>, accessed April 30, 2016.

BARROS, THIAGO - Gear VR, Samsung's virtual reality glasses, gets price in   Brazil- <http://www.techtudo.com.br/noticias/noticia/2015/11/gear-vr-oculos-de- realidade-virtual-da-samsung-ganha-preco-no-brasil.html>, accessed on April 30, 2016.

CHARARA, SOPHIE - The best PlayStation VR games to look forward to - <http://www.wareable.com/sony/best-playstation-vr-games-2016>, accessed April 30, 2016.

Printed by Books on Demand GmbH, Norderstedt / Germany